From a Vein of Lapis Lazuli

From a Vein of Lapis Lazuli

Dakota Minnie Boyer

For Calliope & Circe

"I am the eye with which the Universe beholds itself, and knows it is divine."

-Hymn of Apollo
by Percy Bysshe Shelley

Contents:

Part Two: Echoes & The Oracle

Intro

Be a love and so forever
walk in the veil of tomorrow flushed.
What is justice? Is love
and nothing else so old a story?
Tremble so and all that's truth
know this: I live as my own.

Part One:
Geode Bound

Daybreak

Sweep away all words,
so passed the night-
the fog drew
like mighty cliffs it shaped
and glowering gods watched
like islands mighty and gloomy.
The sun streaked bloody on still water.
The sky, the sea
casing the known past.

18

Standing in line at the airport,
my hands no longer felt my own.
No longer plump with youth,
but delicate as stems of roses.
Turning them this way and that
to see if under the fluorescents
they shown of the five year old
I regressed to be as I clasp hold
of my mother and nodded goodbye
to my father, chasing away tears.
The line moved onward and soon
I was showing ID and passes to TSA,
pushing my backpack along
a conveyer belt, collecting shoes-
knowing when I reached the other side,
I would be on my own.
Westbound, 18.

Silence

Midnight on the eve of spring
snuggled under a too thin blanket,
the night howled its wind-
a silent keeper that tugged upon
the lock of the door.
The deer wandered down
from the mountain as the fog
rolled its way and as I lay
still amongst the calm,
I dare not move to stir
the slumbering love beside me.
My eyes now smudged of tiredness
trace the coyote's stride as he passes
the picture window, down the street-
out from the quietest suburbs
nestled in the heart of Dionysus' fields.
I drew a chilled breath
and shut the door, securing
the lock to keep the ghosts barred
from our dreamer's domain.

A Letter from Psyche's Sister

Do you feel safe under the glow of the moon?
Look close in her waning smile
and see Diana lounging in her craters,
her hounds chasing the stars
across the midnight sky.

Open your eyes.
You are held close by her heart.
Her gaze never leaving your shadow.
Her arrow marks the man who harms you.

Lean into her aid.
Feel yourself among the village of woman
and we will stand by you through the long dark.

You must only light the match.

Namesake

I trace your veil in the portrait
of your wedding day. All the lace
falling in waves like creek water
lapping the shore of Christ's steps.
I imagine the soft patter of your walk
to the altar echoed the way the leaves
blew at the old cabin, gently hugging
sunlight, casting light shadows
on the grass and creek stones.

Your smile beamed sure as Minerva.
Your crown, a shimmering halo in place
of her proud feathers and bronzed helmet.
I'm convinced, if I peer close enough
to collect each fiber of detail, I can almost see
the cherubs hiding amongst the flowers,
disguised as altar boys offering the body and blood.

Dear namesake, I wonder, how am I
ever to fill the shadow of such gods?
If there's an answer, leave the message
imprinted in my skin as I sleep, like
all the other constellations your ghostly kiss
cast to my face, as I lay dreaming
of that black and white photograph
                                            one more time.

6 years

They were a catastrophe
most peculiar. A pair of lovers
swinging on an elementary school
playground at midnight,
singing serenades to Melpomene
until only her voice carried the tune.

She had grown sensitive
in the nights they spent wandering
the streets of the town he grew up.
Feet sore to bleeding on the gravel
path home. He said, it was late.
That she needed to keep walking.
She couldn't help feeling
the way home was growing longer
with each night. That the couch
in the pale green house wasn't
her home, but took a deep breath
and sucked down the thought.
Buried it away for the next night
when they would walk down
this path: past the pizza place,
the street lamps and corner store.

She had envisioned something
more in the way their shadows joined,
but ultimately, she was forced to rupture
as he drove his pain out to bursting-
until she was his injury itself.

The Virgin in the Lion's Den

Pull apart the sky, picture
night as a blur of lazy gods
lounging among their clouds.
Gifted by envy, they remain flushed
by Dionysus' wine, sipping away
at our expense.

You had me by the hand,
told me we'd be going on an adventure.
You pulled me in with myth,
had me imaging the greenery of the forest
flourished by divine hands-
that Pan himself sung in harmony
with the birds. His nymphs played in my shadow
as we wandered ever deeper into the brush.

My free hand tickled ferns through the thick.
I smiled so brightly upon you, as you
led on with determination in your brow.
We stopped at the mouth of a cave
and I laughed, *who am I? Antigone?*
You responded sharp,
I don't know who that is,
leading me nearer the dark.
I beamed, stepping past the threshold,
admiring stalactites, *according to Sophocles-*
Nor do I care. Your tone sharp with rejection,
but still you kissed me softly in that dark,
until the pounding of paws came.

I wonder how long you had dwelled

over the calculation- how long to linger
in tenderness with me. How long was
enough to soften my walls, to lure me out
like the Trojans taking in the horse?
Too long and it would have snatched you too.
Pulled you under its great jaw,
severing breath from us both.

No, you timed it right.
Your lips parted from me the moment
those mighty paws latched on, dragging
me back into the darkness, leaving me
painting moisture like Moses
against the cave floor as you watched on.

You watched as that bloodied snout
made its work to my flesh,
shredding my soul from the bone.
You waited for my surrender,
picking at your fingers as moments drew on,
until finally the lion retreated
from the macabre to tend to his vanity.
And so you left,
not moment more to linger
over the mangled remains.

No pyre awaited me.
No glory like a golden urn.

For all those moments you watched,
tasting pleasure in my blood,
painting stupidity-
gullibility to my constellation,
you missed the serenity of my corpse

as something new emerged from the decay.

Adorned in the tragedy of myself,
I fashioned my armor, forged
the sword from my losses.

As Olympus loomed,
I readied myself for war.

To Converse with Gods

I sit among gods resting
along the halls of Dante's design.
Thinkers of all ages echoing doubt
out to no one- maybe the stars,
but we remain uncertain if they
are willing to listen or if they
cast off our dismay into
the emptiness of space.
Do they stretch out infinity
to sustain all that questioning?

We are caught in the palm
of the greater question:
asking if we're longing to be
or if longing is a place
that we haven't quite reached yet.
I remain content with
leaving it open ended, stumbling
in awe of how shimmering
they remain in this ghostly chamber.

I keep my head low under the gaze of
Nietzsche as Plato paints memory
along the marble. Socrates critiques
the technique in his rushed
finger painting as the thousand
sons of his thought sit stoic beside him.
Each breathing in revelation
upon the sight of their hands.
Each knowing they could never
capture every fiber of Earth within

their cracked dirty palms.

I wonder how gratifying truth must be-
suckling on the ambrosia.

The Long Way Back

The vessel parts a way through the clouds
and I find myself holding your baby fat
fingers with unease growing in my palm.
You smile at the mountains adorned in snow.
They pass below us as frost giants
cradling the south west. I tell you, *that's Colorado*
as your uncle, beside me, laughs
that you won't remember, so
why bother with geography lessons.

I continue,
staring out with you- echoing your coos
in awe of how clear blue the sky is from a bird's eye.
I tell you to trace Helio's chariot, watch
how he pulls the sun along our journey.
Watch him rise as we give away
one coast for another,
vineyards for plantations,
peacocks for alligators.

At last, as the serpentine hips of Florida's
rivers come into view, I breathe
a sigh and tell you, *we're home.*

Loves Lost

The fools should ask of your mask-
of the face it covers, so may love
be none, be gone of here intimate-
burned out like a hundred thousand suns.
But say you want a hundred thousand more,
which is bound, although not
bound by money's worth...
> If then, you will be unsatisfied.
> I will give not, but that seems little,
> for here you demand to have
> and to live, I'd much rather depart.

He Walked Away Israel

I recall to life a blaze
with words open to a passenger.
A secret with no more purpose
than mist closing round
as Selene looked on.

He was a storm shut inside.
The sparks. The light.
A flurry of static tainting June
in feathers, sticky with blood.
A figure caught in his thunderous
flare falls as if in flight,
scattering hope across the field.

I am alone in the mist and darkness,
to wipe mud from face and shake the hate-
standing with the night as he turns
to walk down the hill.

As his figure is at last engulfed
by mist, I blow a kiss to his ghost.
Let it all be gone from my spirit.

Philosopher's Stone

I imagine Flamel hunched
as he pulls forth from geode
that stone of life, glistening golden
of youth and all her bright-eyed lust.

Mama, Mommy, Me

Ten little fingers and toes
gave to me the gift of my title,
highest in all the courts of Europe,
with a kingdom grown to wander,
to conquer, to know that in itself
remains a home laced in their biology.

The doll-likeness I bound close
to my chest adorned my neck
with her arms, and babbled my claim-
mama.

I wore her like pride- proof
to be divine everywhere we would go.
Her straight nose and curious eye
examined new sights as we talked
through our walk.

It's here, I found
the hardened eye staring back.
Determining me to be just another
pair of legs with a lack of piety.
Explicit to insight shame upon me
till I'm shrouded, carted away
like Mary- to treasure my lamb
in the silence of my home.
But I have never been so holy
and you, my bundle, are the craft
of my clay. The birth from my blood.
Born to me and bound to my heart
like a rose bush entangled in my veins.

20

I lifted my head high,
and walked on to savor your coos-
to be the god you made of me.

When You're Old

I think when you're old
you just start hating everything.
Or at least that's the impression
I derive from you, as you coil
your tongue into curses.

I've heard so few beautiful
things flutter out from you that I'm wondering,
are we experiencing the same world?
Am I disillusioned with youth?
With age, do you see the dead walking-
their grotesqueness burning into you
the fragility of flowers?

How can there exist joy among decay?
The men on street corners aren't crazy,
they're just seeing the reality
I have yet to know.
The end is constant in its nearness,
as the sun surely rises.
The radiation baking us slowly-
Tom Lehrer was right when he said
we'd all go together when we go.

Or maybe you're just angry at
everything and
no one but yourself.
Deflecting has always been your strong suit.
All the have nots.
All the should haves- could haves
echo in your ears at night.

Those demons grinding away at an exterior
of sanity until the enamel is finally shed
and you're left raw like a tooth gone bad.
It aches,
so you make the world ache too.

Birth Stone

Hubris is a jealous fire.
Let me be her blaze.
Spark me an explosion of green
to your heart- feel the burn of shame
as you remember how you once told me
I couldn't be the Emerald.

The copper trace
of my untampered pride left
an unappealing tinge to your tongue.
Twisted your smile to approach your goal:
to embarrass me into the submissive Peridot.

I let it go.
May claimed the stone I desired,
leaving August with her quiet twin.
Yet, as weeks fell on, the lion within
me remained dissatisfied by my backdown.
She battered at the cage door.
Clawed at my stomach to set her loose.
Let me show them, she roars.
I can be any gem I want.

She was right.
Nothing so arbitrary as a birthstone
can call to rest the command a lioness
possesses over the blistering sunlight.
Does she look dainty to you?
She's defines a wild fire raging
envious tones in the forests she roams.
She could never be captured

among the glow of a modest gem.

With the forge of her heart inside me
blazing golden, I take hold of the geodes
you stole from me- leaving you weeping
for the worth that was never yours.

Engagement Ring

Stuffed in an ornate box, sheltered by the otherness of
mix matched jewels and birthday finery, rests an
amethyst gem that caught my eye and lingered there
shimmering under the light of an antique store, bathed
in honey and rosemary homemade candles.
At times, I see the twinkling gem embraced by its
sterling lover and think the memories would do well
amongst the deep of the steady river, taken out to sea-
undo the permanence, but then who would I be then
to toss love lost out to sea?
I would be him.

For Future Lovers

Do not reduce me to my body.
It will grow old like the rest, called down
to Hades, faded a little more than dust flirting
with faint light tracing dirty windows.
I am but a summer's night to the Earth,
yet this mind fills in infinity.

You may pluck at the harp of my heart,
but my thoughts remain unfathomable.

Sunflower

Why do you speak to me
as if you hold hot charcoal
on your tongue?

A woman in a wide brimmed sunhat
sets down the book of her affections,
to peer, beyond her balcony,
to the figure sun charred below.
    Excuse me? she asks
    with patrón on her tongue.

Firmly the figure stands,
wielding a weathered watering can.
His arms stretch out, as if capturing
the spirit of wind
flowing through the patch
past him- petals fluttering
with the sun like pits of star flares
caught on earth.
Why do you impart
upon me like a curse?

He twirls, breathing in his work.
You had asked me
to tend to the sunflowers,
yet are displeased to find
them thriving. Is it possible
that I discovered, gratitude has
never been in your vocabulary?
Does it not grip to your heart?
    The woman remains silent,

28

caught in the jaws of annoyance
and boredom. She slowly sips
her drink before standing
as a tower burdened by the air.

Why not wander with me,
among the blossoms, to experience
the success of my labors?
Warmth fills the man's cheeks,
the delight of his work
painting him jolly, in the way
only true joy in one's work could.
He beckons the woman,
to exit her glass coffin house,
to be filled with nature's promise.

She scoffs.
Hand to her mouth,
the chime of her laugh ringing
through silence.
Shock stuns hope from his face.
The man lays down his watering can,
parts a path through the sunflowers,
alone to find enlightenment.

Evening

Sometimes, on hollow days
where I hide like Quasimodo sheltered
among the stained glass of Notre Dame,
I lift the shades to half mass.
Just high enough to trace clouds
across a blissful sky as I lay back against
the pillow and witness the mouth of night
come to swallow the finches flying home-
to see the sky splinter blood orange
before its lover and creator.

In Her Eyes

In her eyes, dark as thunder soaked earth,
I see the storm come to engulf.
I see the rise of white sails against a horizon,
a glittering compass and spyglass passing
sunlight through the mirk of dawn.

In her laugh, light as a bird's love song,
I hear the canopy sing.
The frogs croak in their ponds.
The ambient tune of cicadas offset
by echoes of men yelling across the waves.
Their fingers pointing hungrily to the shore.
Trees swaying under the light breeze.
Hushed tones from locals, hidden amongst shade,
tracing the movements of those bright white sails,
as they come ever nearer the sands.

I hear the discussion in distant tongues,
long forgotten to my lips. I can't dissect
the vocabulary, but from her lips,
I want to scream back through time.
Do not let them land!

In her dance, playful as the sun's peak
through a cloudy sky, I watch our gold jingle
across the sand. I watch the figurines,
the jewelry, the cups pass out from our hands,
like her hands, to be melted down to fill
salt pierced coin purses.

In her dance, I see the last of our pride

stamped out. A flame smothered to ash
by the taste of a Spaniard's greed, painted ruby
on the tips of their swords.

Sacking Versailles

Night:
a mass of black unrolling acute
differences between time- a façade
which looked upon centuries.
It called History a town,
a series of stories- a chapel
to pray to the bourgeoisie.

Be aware,
to awaken means replace
with justice at the center-
not a fatal life destined to birth terror,
not from God, but from man.
And so pressed with the choice,
do I burn my garden in hopes the Earth
retakes her or rip the bulbs by the root?

I let the sun do his bidding
because to be done of you meant
being rid of trying to impress you.

Let night take me to that villa
tracing fingertips on gold,
tasting the heavens before she burns.
Diamonds become nothing
as your divinity never bloomed in mind.

> To depart a stranger was
> a kindness to be free from you.

Your rashness placed you in peril.

I desire heaven and an escape.
Let it be a lesson in judgment.

Do not quarrel with me, my love.
Malice is easy and I am no such enemy.

I've locked your image with the kings
and together you will both burn
till the Earth is but a dizzy blur of ash
swirling so it could be snow.

Fires in the West

Now as the fields of Dionysus burn, she finds herself
fluttering anxious with hope. The imagine of flames
pouring down mountainside to take him is seared to
her conscience. And when she closes her eyes, she can
almost taste his tears of wine mystified, by the heat, till
they're lost like scraps of baby blankets and charred
photo albums.
She feels the hope pull high in her throat to only
plummet in shame. In her mind, his lies were sown to
the soil and with catastrophe it could be renewed.
But still she sees, the cracked earth dry.
Bones charred ash.
The humanity in dusty feet searching what god gave
them as the remainder, the sum of their life when
extracted from flame.
A paradise lost.
She only wished he didn't pluck the blue from the sky-
the water from the leaves.
Leave the good, relinquish the evil.

From Adam's Rib

When she shattered the glass,
the roof caved in like a clamor
bursting the ventricles in his heart.

Adam died and from his rib
grew a thousand wild flowers.
Poppies and Delphinium.

Layers of Revenge

Like Dante, I have travelled through
the cave with a curse upon my tongue-
casting hexes from my pen.
But that was only layer one.

That was the anger boiling beneath me,
fueling the pyre of my own burning-
my self damnation,
so I may cast you as the player I suited.
When we are long gone, someone else will say,
what did they do to make her so mad?

I'm choosing to bury the remaining keys,
to hold back my curiosity to venture
further below, to follow the coil down
to the bottom and watch that frostbitten beast
chewing Iscariot's spine.

No, I will let you burn in your own time,
by your own hand. In your inferno,
I will look on with that smirk of narcissism
against my lips and say, *of all the wicked things*
I've let my heart become, there still remains
one thing worse than me,

you.

A Word with the Night

So woo not the world.
In truth, fair night,
I'll prove more cunning
in true love's passion.

Pardon me, yielding night
so discovered by blessed moon
that tips silver.
I swear not by Selene,
her love is variable-gracious

                                  with no joy.

Dream

Dreaming, a far faint star
burned fierce and wild
broke the quiet of youth,
as she streaked across a twilight
bliss sky masterfully silver,
sprinkling stardust as she went.

Along came Growth
golden in splendor from his birth,
and Fear shook the forest.
That painted jade boy crawled
out from a nightmare to ball his fists
and bellow at the skies,
while we wait for our forlorn dream.

Growth took hold of Fear and
said only this, *together we
can make something beautiful.*

To Converse with Gods

Part 2

It is here,
     in the grasp of 3am
     sleeplessness-
     fighting against agony
     I've traced into the ceiling
     above my bed,
I understand the thief.
How he stood upon the hill,
eyeing the ladder,
ready to grapple with gods.

For if I found such a tear in time,
I would pull through to wage war
upon the divine hiding beyond such a veil.
I'd dare him to once again walk in the present.
To live death's desire and find, as Camus found,
the invincible summer blazing on
in the depths of winter.
To hear him say, upon revelation,
I'm sorry,
for all the trials,
the plot twists,
the sleepless nights cast against void,
the nightmares twisting the psyche.
I'm sorry.
Come back down my path.

I remain, struggling against air,
searching for the seam to strangle silence.

Exotic

Standing in line at checkout,
I heard his desperation tone.
His yearning for a vision of Spanish gold-
a dark haired curve he could bring
under his Christian tongue.

I wish I had spoken, to call out my disgust.
To say a woman is exotic, is to say
she's unknowable in your ignorance.
You wish to tame the wild from her hair,
her full tooth grin, pluck the color
from her skin and wear her among your kin.

But a woman is not a fur.
We are not the tigress in the forest.
We are not the feather of a peacock,
nor the heat of the jungle.
We are regal in our temper
and tire of your wolf whistle.

So chime again,
how exotic us Latin girls are and see how
American blood tastes in your mouth.

The Cab Scene

Early autumn, he wandered in,
not like humble leaves shed, but
as if he was the god of leaves himself.

I welcomed him.
Had him pull up a chair
to share in the discussion,
but he was more inclined to
view the world from the tip
of his nose, as if our poetry
poured too modern for his
sweet tea.

That southern boy thought
himself Hemmingway or Faulkner
with an air of Trump, blessed by
the one true god to share
his Aryan wisdom with
the rest of us.

Month after month after month
he came to recite heartbreak
he would never recover from- to tell
of the gargoyle within him, the beast
waiting for his true love's kiss
and I internally vomit void again
and again, as I feign kindness,
hoping he'll go away.

But he never does.
Instead, he leans in too close,

peers down at my chest with his mouth
gaped open like a hungry coy.
I gag when he says *I don't know*
whether to be afraid or turned on.

I rather he be afraid.

I leave each meeting reminded
of Audrey caught in the cab, with
a too eager suitor playing out symbiosis
and I know, I don't want to live my life
like Breakfast at Tiffany's.
When caught in the cab, I want to jab
his catcalls back down his throat
till the bile spills out his eyes.

It's near winter now.
He comes again.
I welcome him in to pull up
a chair to share in the discussion.

He sits too close, mouth
watering agape as he eyes
my crossed arms and solid gaze.
I imagine, he envisions me
as a muse he can't let get away.
As he sees the love beside me, he scoffs.

I read my allegory to his hero's ego,
feeling plates of earth shift
under my words as I call him out.
He shudders upon my unveiling,
pulling apart his heart-stricken façade
for what it is: a full grown toddler

whose mother never weaned
from the entitlement bound
in baby fat fists screaming
at the top of his lungs about
all lives matter and *not all men*.

I watch him play victim in his skin,
as if the blood on the hands
of his brothers in white poured
from their own fatten necks
and not brown boys they stole
from mothers arms as they beat
a life senseless on the pavement,
to laugh as their mothers claim
their boys will be boys.

He chose the wrong woman
to prey on. I stand, looming over
the mess of him and skin his pride
from his fat and cook the fat from
the bone till he's a shivering skeleton,
pitiful in dismay.

He walks away
and I shudder by the ghostly touch
of the ancestors before me
that never got the chance
to fillet the white man.

Hubris

Cupid struck as I waged war
with Apollo, so sure of his arrow,
I couldn't see the shadow of the past
plucking upon its constellation
till his form arose before me.

And Zeus laughed at my plight
to conquer the stars
when I couldn't control my heart.

Song of the Heart

Eyes closed
hands outstretched,
you produced the geode of my heart.
Rough & unrefined-
extracted from my chest.
You said, the pride of my emerald core
could be worth something or
                                        nothing at all.
You said, to tune my ear
for hidden gems instead-
those small, yet incomparable.
The sun can only guess the reason why,
in infinity's first cry, time embedded
a star trilling within me.
It will be years before
its song erupts a symphony.

Haunting

Transcending the known,
diving into the primal
cased in the clouds looming
ever lower upon the earth.
It's as if the atmosphere dared embrace
her tighter, to shed his affection
until it became this mass of heart
where reality warps like split glass.
A black mirror with no bottom.

We drove through fog
and for a moment I grew unsure,
feeling the night- the highway
of another place years past
between the mountains,
when the Lands of Dionysus
flushed of youth- when I was drunk
on his wine and believed
I could wander to Olympus' peak.

I had been wrong then as I was now,
but still my body contorts in anxious breaths.
As the clouds part along the drive,
I recognize street lamps, bumps in
the sidewalk and leave the ghosts
of my mind to wander into the fog alone.
Let the clouds keep them.

Part Two:
Echoes & The Oracle

To the Fates

Paint me on the canvas of destiny.
Tell me where I am to settle-
where to lay the sword in the snow,
let it caress me to sleep,
buried like a dream.

Night Haunter

More than I can say,
I've dreamed a face familiar,
but none I can name.

Each time I happen upon their path,
they catch me and I know them,
while the tug of my consciousness
consistently wonders how...

Could they be my past,
some old face echoing to me
from a cave I had long since forgotten I left?
Plato, tell me, how could a shadow seem complete?
Seemingly fixed in marble, a statue
I know each curve of.
The sculptor so precise, I place Medusa's work.
Such a phantom must only exist in
the imagination of twilight- tangible as dew.
They are never more than a moment's reflection
I wish to grasp on to
                    and never let go,
yet the dream still fades.
Their palace lost to the caverns of my mind.

To Be Her Mother

I roll over to find her curled beneath my blankets. Her
little nose poking out as her doll like eyes remain
closed to dream of fairies and conquest. It is here, in
the stillness as the cat darts through the curtain,
tossing light into the room, that I feel no matter the
nightmares I battle in the night, I remain her
lighthouse. And in the pit of the night, when she wakes
alone, she knows she's safe along my shores, to snuggle
beside me until the light urges her awake, to smile.
"Good morning, Mommy."

Iliad

They strode through a crimson field,
painted merciful by a golden pride
anchored around them like a forlorn halo.
Their hands joined by whispered
vows to never part another's arms, words
they sung to another's soul in stolen glances
and later, kisses aboard an eastbound vessel.
        [All the earth,
        this misadventure abounds
        with lovesick dreamers proclaiming
        history has never written a better story.
        Yet, did they envision the carnage-
        the untold price for such a cause?]

With each step she took from shore
to gate birthed decay, marked blood
across the sand and soiled vineyards.
Hecuba gripped Priam tight, envisioning
the sons tossed from towers, eyeing
high spirited Hector and his flushed bride
as they watched the lover's parade through the gates.

You'd think, by the light in Aphrodite's eyes,
crafting the gold in Helen's hair, that Paris
would see the wake of a thousand ships in her smile.
Odysseus might reason, he was caught
by the allure of her siren hips, but even
as Paris lay slain by Menelaus' sword,
                he leans into fate.
The blade alone burdened to haul
the soul of a prince away, leaving Menelaus

unsatisfied as he wipes the sword clean
with the Trojan's claim resting on his tongue
for the remainder of his life.
There is no end to us.

On the Boardwalk with You

Staring into the night, I feel for once visible-
a speck illuminated by a laugh and a story.
A shooting star grazes the sky as we conjure
the past, reminiscing those ghosts to the present.

And I feel here, on the boardwalk,
under the gaze of Orion, his bow arched
by Cupid's command. But I don't kiss you.
I don't lean into the warmth of your embrace
or rest my mind upon your shoulder.

We stare out at the horizon, painting
the topography of our city, content to share
our words with someone who will hear them
and laugh unapologetic as the waves
lap the shore and the ghosts we know
depart for the future to begin.

Sleeping Beauty

Dream a forgotten fairytale:
    Adorned in honesty, shown through
    Earth moss eyes and a laugh ever present
    in the corner of his smirk, he approaches
    the castle, sure he will be the one.

    Though marked by the dark, he sees
    a flicker of candle in the highest window.
    He makes aim with courage,
    to see what's present beyond the murk
    and decay of princes married to the burden
    of death, their skeleton's gripping tight
    to shields long lost of any promised glory.
    He sheds his pride,
    striding towards the briar without armor,
    without sword, without a notion of how
    to be anything but what he is- curious.

    To his surprise, the thorns break.
    He finds his shadow against stone,
    wandering along the expanse of corridors
    moonlit throne rooms, along the curve
    of tower stairs spiraling into the heavens.
    The hope before him a dream,
    a whisper at his ear, it draws him on
    till at last he stands where the princess lies
    and she smiles, knowing all along
    someone would brave the journey.

Self Portrait at a Dinner Party

The following are the varying
shades of isolation I find myself painted.

> *Cobalt*:
> We walk in and I am
> a figure standing against
> the crashing sea. A rock blessed
> by a seafoam kiss, eroded with
> each cycle of moon, snow pierced
> white by the sun's gaze. Like an
> earth forged lighthouse, that's
> desperate to flee the coast.

> *Ruby:*
> Lips spread tight
> in a line- the horizon at sunset,
> sighing away light as it recalls
> it's place as the backdrop to a lover's
> breathless kiss from neck
> to hips. The dress tight
> to the body attached to
> yours by a soft hand on the back,
> a head against the shoulder
> and an on cue laugh.

> *Chestnut*:
> Eyes searching a crowd
> for a face that sees my own.
> For a voice to ask something
> about me- to save me from
> the silence I find myself in

as you make small talk
over business, to reassure me
that I'm not just arm candy.
I'm franticly searching
in the room full of people
I'll never know for someone
to look just right of you
and ask my opinion.

But I'm drowning
like the falscly buricd.
Casket lid collapsed and
I'm desperate to climb
out, but how? Where is
the sky? I can't breathe.

Midnight:
Numb as moonlight
trapped in a tomb of cumulus,
the static at toes from
lack of circulation.
I wait- buy my time picking
at fingernails in my lap
as I listen idly to the chatter
like static on, what we used
to refer to as, the snow channel
on bad weather days.

Detached.
I'm in the car.
I breathe.
I'm in my bed.

It's over, but the pit of midnight

stays tight to my lungs
till I purge in the night
tears against pillowcase.
Mascara smears while you're asleep.

Honey:
And you're asleep,
breathing softly as if stress
cannot touch
your subconscious mind.
I lean into your chest,
waiting to grow warm again
in my dreams.

Catfish

Florida boy, with a craftsman's smile,
tossed out a line to wheel me in.

I witness his joy, only to ache
with the tar bit thought tugging
at the back of my throat till I'm heaving
with guilt- how you'll toss me back again
once you see, I'm not the rainbow
scaled sea maid you believed me to be.
Or worse, how you'll keep me.
Let the mistake on your heart
weigh you down into the bog,
for you to become another artifact,
to remind me I was made to destroy.

Patroclus

The ferryman calleth with beckoning finger,
a bitter that woes endure mark the dark-
a blaze of eyes. In anguish and pain,
love most shares in grief.
There is no strength left in my feet as I linger
ever nearer the night, darkening down.
Kiss my farewell to light, so I may look blessed,
though to nothing I am, for your word
rusheth o'er me passing by the gods-
if our hearts are a shrine in our passing,
thou seest all my plight, would I speak
mine heart's wish, honoring thee before
my own soul, unconstrained for thee?

I might have dwelt crowned,
yet would not live torn away from thee.

The Storyteller

With a careful smile, you told me
you had a story for every situation.
You could pull them from a dark cellar of brain,
speak the remembrance as a painting
and I, an admirer of art, witnessed the paint
strokes form before me, to stand in awe
as they echo every emotion as an invocation to Apollo.

He rides by your command,
the daughters of Mnemosyne following behind,
their skirts fluttering with their dance.
You are an oracle,
and I hang on your every vision.
The moonlight wavered along the water
from their light footsteps and as you hung
over the edge, head to the dark-
you shone Selene's light as the next story began.

And it's in this moment that I begin to wonder,
great wordsmith, how will our story end?
Will we erupt Vesuvius or fade an ellipsis
tinkering out into infinity's bliss?
In your words, how do you see me?
Do you paint me a partner, friend or accomplice?
Call upon your divinity and show me-
stop the motion of the wind, impose upon the rain-
a girl unmovable as earth,
rich in expression and a laugh that stuns the dark.
In all other stories, I am small,
but I wonder to you, am I divinity herself?

True Love

They have come side by side
to watch blind- listening
for hope yet to come.

Her fingers tangle among his,
as vines desperate to overtake
an old brownstone. She wishes
to distinguish her feelings, away
from a weed, to something to be
adorned with. Something on lookers
could gawk over longingly, as she had
so often seen, as she sat watching
HGTV alone, with a kitten nestled
in the curve of her neck as a scarf.

She wonders, if he is her house,
her fairytale ending, her romcom
foot popper firework maker-
true love, if there was such a thing.
Though, as time draws on
through aisles in the cathedral,
the hymns found their last note.
The only congregation remaining
in the pews are that of her fears.
They turn to her with gaping
mouths spewing tar, *when do you think*
it'll be that his love will shatter as
fractured first sunlight?
When he looks upon your sleeping face,
will he burn or wither?
What will you craft him to be

when you forge the lie?

Gripping his hand,
the tears catch her throat.
She urges *let's go*
and runs on, not waiting for reply.

Achilles

His comrades go out to battle. The rumble of a golden chariot charging a way through the sun burnt sand, the light eclipsed by a flick of a feathered helmet, bronze men echoing Ares' cry, thirsty for a clash of metal and wit. Only today, part of his bravery broke, having been confronted with the choice between pride and country, he unknowingly sacrificed love.

Pacing his tent, he hears the distant roar as an ocean of men lay themselves down upon the earth, but he thinks nothing of them. He doesn't imagine how the same faces of youth which had cheered his name that first damning day before the war, now release their souls upon the sword of the enemy he knows he should be fighting. He doesn't linger on the resentment they must feel. The abandonment. The thrown hands to echo the cries, that the gods have truly left them, as not even their fabled hero will fight.

He leaves his tent for the shore, marking his way through the sand. The sudden boom of renewed strength bounds down from the battlefield. He imagines his glimmering love clad in armor fit only for a sea nymph's son. The feathered helmet alone driving the Greeks back into formation, to push the son's of Priam back into their crumbling city. He does not worry, he instead releases his shoulders from burden- the weight from his jaw as he walks into the shallows. He thinks *the fight can carry on without me. Let me linger, ever near the horizon, to collect more years.*

If only.

The craftsmanship of fate cannot be diverted, it instead stows away like a rat bound for the new world.

It's here in the shallows, his sea dark mother catches his eye, having risen from the palaces below to cry salt tears. He hears the rush of his men calling his name. He feels his heart ache until it becomes the ashes filling up a golden urn. He knows before she speaks.

    "The After will hold him."

Human

We remain
a desperate attempt of flesh,
fighting against air,
surrounded by the love
we do not recognize,
until slowly that love is consumed.
Only their ashen ghost survives.

Kindness

Wandering along a maze of capitalist delights, neon followed by loud music, perfumes and distant teen laughter, you make your way to the dressing room. Few garments in hand, but only one can come home with you. That's all you'll allow yourself.

You've been told to give, but the execution has always lingered along the abstract. You pretend to be a treat yourself person- self rewarding, adorning yourself in packages on the 'gram. Yet, when the few purchases make their way to your door, you hide them, stuff them behind pillows to awe over the texture of packaging before it must go swiftly to the recycle bin- no one must know you bought something new for yourself. The thought of their thoughts buzzing wildly with judgement is dizzying.

Now you're here, standing alone in the changing room, clothes on the fancy store hangers. You peer into the mirror that you're convinced belongs in a funhouse. Each time, you seem smaller, less real than the last time, as if you're shrinking away from criticism.

This is your reflection, begging the question, is it safe or satisfying to compare yourself with all others- to say, you do not deserve this because you do not have the luxuries of another, until you've beaten yourself into the pit in your chest you've long tried to sew shut?

Look at me.

Look at you.

Recognize each are made of silver stardust and if you choose to be, you may open the world's ear to any mind.

Revisiting that Feeling

Head to sky, feet in the water.
I wait for him to call.
Silly as a child,
it's been so long since I felt
the breeze blow kindness
and the sun gaze longingly from his perch.
I hope not to be another song for Apollo.
Imagining him at his lyre, plucking
a laugh with his fingertips- cruel.

Yet, I feel I am the sea, floating
to nowhere and not minding.
I promised myself I'd never write
a love poem, but then I heard his serenade.
Thoughtful are his words, sensible as Selene.

Drifting away,
I realize, I don't mind this one.
Let them laugh.

Hector

The Trojans had advanced across the plain, reclaiming their land as they went-pushing the Greek army so far to the shore, they would soon be casting off from the coast or burning with their sails. As word arose like a gossiping howl, how Achilles divorced himself from the sword, strength grew in Hector's men. Years they had been cooped within their walls, peering out to view the desolation of burnt groves and vineyards, but now they dared to dream- to see their sons toddling under the canopy, to collect apples and feel the coast's kiss to their feet.

It's here in the height of their victory, in full blessing of Aphrodite, that their day dreams shattered as the neighboring sacked cities, like pottery flung messily out of windows and silk torn from a woman's skirt. The battle cries. The unmistakable trill of the Myrmidons and as they crested the plain, outline of his helmet against the sun scorched the very souls of the Trojans, that had over the past days seen courage grow at the tip of their swords.

Some ran. Hector couldn't blame them. It was Achilles out for his birthright, his honor among their blood. But Hector drew his breath like a prayer to Apollo. *Guide me in this to bring my men home.* Rallying the men he could among the chaos, Hector pushed through the Greeks, plowing away at their exhaustion until the golden helmet with the pompous display of feather was in sight. He was sure to rip off the tuff and bring the foolish boy within down from his pedestal- to show his men just how weak the best of the Greeks was- to reignite their spirits to see the war through. Push the Greeks to their boats. Force them to sail home.

But as he neared Achilles' chariot, it turned to flee, sparking an anger in the pit of Hector's chest. *How dare he come only to give into cowardice.* He ran ever faster, feeling the spirit of the gods guiding his movements. He grabbed a spear and threw with greater strength than Heracles, than Ajax, than all of them and laughed when the chariot crumbled. The rush. The silence as the Trojans drew around him. The shock from the Greeks. The best had been downed. Slowly he bounded his way to the form crawling out from the sand. His hand testing the weight of another spear before throwing. There was no way he was letting Achilles run away now. *Become the man you were born to be,* he thought. The spear connected with chest and the body fell faint like an escape, like the soul was being chased away.

Looming above the form, Hector gripped the helmet by the tuff and hoisted it overhead. The praise was deafening from his men. Achilles finally dead, though a true disappointment it was to see the man was less than his myth. *Was this truly a god?* he thought. Though he was but the son of a nymph, Hector expected something more from the slain- some glow to his skin, some tone to his body, not the scrawny crooked nosed boy that lay before him.

It was then, he knew his deed. It was in the way the Myrmidons collected their dead. The stone of their eyes cold and the distant weeping from Aphrodite. The displeasure of lover's torn from another's embrace. Both armies halted their rage, carted home with a knowing eye upon the other. The silence laid thick across the plain. Only for a moment had Hector heard the godly clamor radiate through to his chamber that night and nothing after. Not a sound. The wind itself had departed for the despair. It was as if he felt his thread growing taut for Atropos' doing.

He knew to savor this night caught in Andromache's arms. To remember the smell of lavender in her hair. The smile of her sleep. Yet he found himself debating in his sorrow, which he would miss more, the sleeping love beside him or the chunky baby hand clasp tight to his finger and the innocence of his dreams. As morning arose before him, he found he could not decide.

The rattle of a chariot drew his attention towards the end, towards his armor, towards the gates of the city and away from the warmth of his bed. He drew his peace with the gods, their ways, their indifference to mortal suffering and gave himself to destiny.

In his final moment, before the chaos drew him in, he laughed at his foolishness- his idiocy to believe the man he had killed could be in any imagination a figure head for the beast before him. With eyes forged from the depths of the sea, Achilles rivaled the stare of Medusa.

Hector looked at him with a gloom held deep.
Am I of earth and blood?
Am I only a rider of blood flowing from his vanity?

The One Who Came Before

They say you're full of grace,
gifted by merciful hands.
Hands that held the blade
to his neck, gently applying pressure
till he cried out all his humanity.
You turned love into shackles.

You missed the lessons in the sermon—
to love another as you'd want love in return.
Instead, you sit head down in the pews,
scissors in hand, snipping away psalms
to suit your patchwork faith.
But where in the Bible do they say
it's ok to rip a man of his self-worth?
Did not Samson cry when Delilah cut
from him his mane, his strength—
the divinity torn from him until
the glimmers of heaven grew obscured.
A night so sure, you'd never believe in the sun's return.

And still you sing in that crow
cracked voice the hymns. But I can see
the demons in the shadows of your palm,
beckoning another to your blood-stained bed,
to be clawed in their sleep by insecurities
you kept chained for a fortnight—
just long enough to become accustomed
to the creaks and moans of the floors.
It's an old house, you said, filled with the nightmares
you drew alliances with, peeking out from cobwebs
and hallowed scriptures until time draws

them ready to pounce, to gouge the eyes clean
from sockets as you hoist the hair, a sinful flag-
the sigil of your clan.

Cargo

She was on a voyage of affection,
hope and happiness determined to preserve.
A hasty scrawl of knowledge,
drawn recluse by a hard series of circumstances.
Her lips bound shut with the memory
of sufferings inconsiderable.
How the past left a malicious shadow
lingering along the shades, peaking in
at moonlight to draw up the covers
and force itself upon her skin
till the impression bled.

> [These are things that crash through
> her consciousness like a mudslide
> waiting to suffocate in her sleep-
> smothered beneath blankets
> desperate to hide.]

She lay beside him pushing
the tragedy back down her throat,
breathing slow as she traces his freckles.
They're enveloped by the cool night
seeping up from the old floors,
with a stillness accompanied by a chorus
of snores from small ones snoozing down the hall.

It is here, she closes her eyes to faceoff
with her abyss growling anxiety through
her veins till it burns.

> *When I tell you,*
> *I've endured winter to a fire,*
> *know I will not trouble you.*

He pulls her in, blowing out the flame
as his lips caress of her shoulder.
They lay together nestled in a warm love,
like a cargo at sea bobbing just off the coast.
He breathes in her hair.

> *Among the many extraordinary things,*
> *there is you.*

Return

I felt steady on the edge of infinity
holding your ring in my palm.
I wonder if you felt the same
pounding of heart as you gripped
the amethyst I tasked you to throw
or if it truly felt like air passing
through you, falling away like baby fat.

We'll throw on three, you said
with eyes searching my face
for uncertainty bound in my brows
and a slight frown, but I held none.
I was ready the moment you told
me how years ago you stood alone
on a ship bound for northern Europe,
realizing in the quietness of summer
that you were no longer heartbroken.
How you slipped her promise ring
from your finger like a sin shed in confessional,
let it fall out of grasp till it was gone,
and felt nothing.

I wanted to know your indifference,
so when we counted down that night
on the boardwalk, I threw with all the
love I had left and felt the weight
of that simple amethyst ring
shed from me, as if the water was
Heracles ready to grip the world for me-
to let me return to your embrace
with no one left between us.

To Converse with Gods
Part 3

Come back, Time and spend a few hours.
Give my love to them, I am sorry.
I cannot stay, said Time.
Morning is on her way, for she will sing,
but tell them, she added, *that when I return,*
I will stay... though I don't know when.
The Spring will come and sing her
love for those gone of you.
Turning home, having paid a visit-
you wont forget my love, will you?

Peace of Dreams

*(from a blackout poem
of Walt Whitman's "Leaves of Grass")*

Beautiful as they lie,
they flow the earth east
to west, hand in hand–
hand in hand.

Her lover close with his lips
press her neck, with measureless love
and breath goes with breath.
Friend unarmed by friend.
The wronged made right.

Step fourth relieved.
The head is free and passages
o   p   e   n.
Become awake to themselves,
in the night and the night awake.

I too pass, but I return to you
and am not afraid.

A Quiver & Bow

Golden was Apollo, his touch
glittered with metallic traces of heaven
leaving my hand adorned as he steadied
my bow- counseling the arrow to strike.

He sang to me, calmed the jolt in my chest
into a steady thunder, reminding me
of the shape of my brother-
how he was carted behind the chariot
till the skin peeled away, leaving only
the memory of an older sibling's displeasure.

I saw it the moment I strode through our gates
with the prize of Aphrodite laced to my heart.
I saw it in his glance out to sea,
in how he distanced joy- partook less and less
of my company, in the way he donned
his helmet out to battle, in the way he shone
of the sun's rage in our privacy amid corridors,
in the way he spit at her feet, prayed the gods
we not be cursed, in the way he said
pick up your sword and fight
and in his withdrawal when he knew I couldn't.

I saw it in the way he went through the gates
to sacrifice himself to the beast, in the way
his body lay in defeat, dusted from the duel,
in the way the soul fell away, as his skin
fell away, as our hope fell away.

As I studied the warrior married to blood,
I saw the fight in his eyes illuminating destruction
and knew to let go,
let the arrow find it's match–
to be better than a crook crowned prince.

Skeleton

The bonfire bellowed
as it swallowed the tree whole.
The beast within the flames
insatiable in its hunger-
blew the flames black and
rushed us with heat astounding the soul.
How what once stood proud among
the pines of the west gave way
so willingly to ash, as if knowing
in our life's end we must bow
to the great dark- may we go
as a serenade or a battle cry.

I watched the embers flicker
into the pitch of night caught
by Selene's palm and wondered a moment,
holding tight to your arm as an anchor,
if I let go, maybe I'd float away too.
Or would you grip me tight-
pull me back into the Earth's
tender embrace, as you had that morning
as we stood on the lawn, drenched in sweat
and dirt, as you lowered her body into the grave.
She never asked to return to soil,
but you knew no other place
would belong to her more...

> and so I wonder,
> when the embers take me,
> will you be there plucking
> my soul back down from air-
> intangible-

abstracted for good.
A fractal of a fractal.
The skeleton of a Christmas tree
on December 29th.

Sparkler

A beacon in the night.
A light to mark the dark
to lead the soul of the year
to pass through fingertips of time,
leave only ripples in skin-
the wrinkles on the face
of a nameless god
robed to collect the year.
                    So pass we all.

Siren Song

Wandering to find the source
of the serenade stringing
through my lungs-
the waves surging to the sound.
My boots trudge through mud.
The dandelions I used to wish on
remain unfulfilled.
I imagine myself coasting
among sea life as the foam
from wince I came.
I urge the sun to take me back-
Mesozoic and ancient as his sunrise.
He sets and I am alone,
cold as January whispers through Florida.

I am alone, kicking my feet,
swinging on a swing-set for two.
Did you know I was missing?
How long was I caught by the siren's song,
held back by the salt sprayed
seat of this bench, holding back urges
gasping at serenity?
How long were you without me
and apathetic to my departure?

This agony burnt deep into my flesh
has been carried for years
and years more I will remain
trudging along the mud, dragging
the corpse of stone behind me,
never to throw into the sea

to be buried.

I wander back to you,
feeling a ghost, as you give
but a quiet recognition of longing,
unaware I heard the song of the sea
and left my soul with her.

Achilles Beyond the Grave

I walked in the echoes of Ulysses' footfalls,
through the fog, hung black along the lagoon.
My grip leaving sweat on the coins he had given me,
from Minerva, to buy my way through the dark.

Do not speak to the Ferryman, he had said.
His hands firm as the grave, sensible to belong
to a killer. I wondered, how many deaths
it would take to relinquish his thread, as I crept
into the cave with only his words to haunt me.
Simply go and come back.
See what I have seen.

Charon pockets the coins for Hades' vault
as I board his vessel salt pierced cold,
to sit among a dread- nameless in their despair.
I wonder if they all come this way or was
Patroclus weeping as Hector sat stoic beside him.
If they came together at all.

I felt a longing in the way the river flowed,
gently patting the boat's side,
almost beckoning me to dip a finger-
to feel the coax of the dark linger
on my skin like wax, but I did as Ulysses said.
I played an intruder to foolishly blend,
full knowing the eye of Hades
followed my shadow, forced to remain
only a figure head lounging
on a throne of bones as the Fates
pulled the needed threads into play,

diverge to paint the story.

Charon drew on as he had centuries before,
indifferent as he parted a path by Cerberus' paw.
I found myself in awe of how ever a beast
so forged in darkness could ever be
sung to sleep by a man and his lyre-
how any chain could bind him-
how any man could stare into those ember
eyes and not break away all remaining strength,
to not wither and die again.

Soon we had been carried into the isles,
where the murk parted and those marked
with little fortune departed- letting their feet
dip into the shallows, to make acquaintance
with what promises the meadow could give them.
I alone wandered into Elysium.
I alone felt the warmth of sand,
the warmth of a world in the absence of sun,
to let my hands part the tall grass,
to find him sitting alone plucking
the song of his demise from his golden lyre.

He's as handsome as they say.
There's no mistaking the divine craftsmanship
of his jaw or in how the light haloed him.
But the way the green of his eyes grew dark
in my gaze, his beauty faded.

> And in mockery,
> our minds were bent upon vengeance.
> I was a hero, long ago taken to Troy.
> Treasure carried the key to greatness.

A quiver and bow.
Now time has come for me
to make a man from you.

I held his verse in the pit of my heart
like a curse, recognizing the thorn I carried
all along, to feel the burden in his gaze.

I was wrong to go, to be carried
by the weight of another man's lust.
I was wrong to fight
for the guilt of my glory.

It's from here, I release the tenseness
in my chest, to walk back onto the boat,
to be born from another vein,
to feel Hades' wrath as I let go of my revenge.
I choose to sail on.

From the Forge

Her journey
had taken away her breath.
For a minute, in silence, she recovered
sitting among the ashes-
looking into the fire,
as if she was a question.

March 20ᵗʰ, 2018

On a spring afternoon,
we stood in the hall as my heartbreak
spilled forth from my chest, caught
in my throat, eyes swollen from the tears.
You just love with your whole heart, she said
as she rubbed away the weight of
the cosmos crashing upon me.

Through spring,
Through summer,
Through autumn,
Through winter,
I searched for the shards of myself
that shattered the day he lied
with a smirk on his lips.

Like Jove, he scattered himself
along the earth in indifference,
leaving the question hanging
from a broken sky: what did I expect?

Even as spring comes to kiss
upon the neck of the south again,
I do not know.

I remain a fallen star trilling through
the night, born from a vein of Lapis Lazuli.
When caught by the grasp of love's
longing eye, I give up all I can-
shimmering in the palm of unworthy hands.

Light

Revolving the expanse,
I hear his satellite serenade
erupt from the dark, calling me
back home to fall through
the atmosphere into arms dreamy-eyed
as dew drops on dawn adorned leaves.

Brushing ice from my hair,
the astronomer kisses my stars-
outlines my galaxies
before stepping away struck.
> *I am just a speck*
> *in awe of your majesty.*
To me, he was a constellation
unto his own, streaked by heartbreak
and a clever laugh that could breathe
life into the coldest of stars.

In that moment,
I may have been his universe,
but he was the light.

Glossary of Gods Heroes Beasts & Terminology:

Greek & Roman

Achilles- declared the greatest fighter in his generation, Achilles was a demigod known for his involvement and drama in Homer's Iliad. Having refused to fight for the Greeks as having disagreed with Agamemnon's politics, he only returned to the battlefield after his lover Patroclus stole his armor and was subsequently murdered by Hector on the field. He sought revenge for his lover's death by utterly destroying Hector in hand to hand combat. He then dragged Hector's body behind his chariot in disrespect. Achilles was ultimately defeated by Paris, who shot an arrow through his heel. In the Odyssey, Odysseus visits Achilles at the pool of the dead, where he expresses a deep regret for living fast and dying young.

Ambrosia- the nectar of the gods. It was believed to grant immortality.

Ajax- one of the many Greek heroes to travel to Troy to fight to bring Helen back to Sparta. He was depicted with a godly stature, towering over most men with the courage to match.

Andromache- a Trojan princess married to the ill-fated hero, Hector.

Antigone- the daughter of Oedipus and his mother, Jocasta. In Sophocles' play of the same name, she is sentenced to be buried alive in a cave for giving proper burial rites to her brother. Her uncle, the new ruler after the demise of Oedipus, decreed that her brother was to be shamed and bared from receiving the rites, thus making Antigone's action treason. She stands by her decision when questioned and accepts her punishment.

Aphrodite/ Venus- the goddess of beauty and mother of Cupid. She was born from sea foam following Cronus' defeat of his father, Uranus. She had many escapades with mortals and gods. She is most notable for helping start the Trojan war in Homer's Iliad. She gifts Helen to Paris as a reward for him saying she was the most beautiful goddess, thus ending a feud started by Eris (goddess of discord.) Out of all the gods, she was the only Olympian to immediately side with the Trojans in the war.

Apollo- the twin of Artemis, he was the god of the arts (music, poetry, visual arts) as well as prophecy, knowledge, archery and the sun (among many other things.) He was the god invoked by the Oracle of Delphi (otherwise known as Pythia.) He pops up time and time again in mythology, most notably in Homer's Iliad, where he makes a solid stance against the Greeks after blatant disrespect is shown to his priests and their families. He ultimately aids Paris in his slaying of Achilles.

Ares- the god of war, specifically the violent carnage. He was depicted as riding into battle with his twin sons

Phobos (fear) and Deimos (terror) beside him in the chariot. He fathered both (along with many others) with his lover, Aphrodite.

Athena/ Minerva- the goddess of wisdom, war strategy and justice (among many other things.) She appears in many myths, though most notably she aided Odysseus in Homer's Iliad and Odyssey, as she favored the Greeks in the Trojan War.

Cerberus- the three headed dog charged with guarding the underworld, to stop the dead from leaving.

Charon- the ferryman of the underworld. The recently dead paid him in coins, which were placed on their bodies during traditional burial rites, so they may board his boat and be ferried across the rivers Styx and Acheron into the isles of the afterlife. He often ferried still living heroes into the afterlife as part of a overarching theme in Greek mythology known as catabasis mytheme.

Cupid- the son of Venus/Aphrodite and Mars/Ares. He was the god of love and affection. He is most notable in the myth of Cupid and Psyche.

Diana/Artemis- goddess of the hunt, forested areas, protector of women, the moon, and archery. She was the twin of Apollo. In myth, she vowed to remain a virgin and was one of the few gods invocated to aid women in childbirth.

Dionysus- the god of wine, viticulture, fertility, resurrection, theatre (among many other things.)

Culturally speaking, he is one of the oldest worshipped gods in ancient Greek culture. With the Cult of Dionysus dating back to the Mycenaean Civilization at the end of the Bronze Age (approximately between 1600-1100 BCE.) Due to this, his depiction has changed over the centuries from an older bearded man to that of a more youthful androgynous figure. Culturally, he was understood to be, in many ways, a protector of the social outsider.

Elysium- in one interpretation of the ancient Grecian and Roman afterlife, Elysium was the island reserved for fallen heroes.

The Fates- the three goddesses of life, destiny and death. Clotho, the weaver of the thread of life, controlled the central points to a person's being, like when they were born etc. Lachesis, the measurer of the thread, controlled destiny. Atropos, the cutter of the thread, controlled how someone died and when the time came (as decided by Lachesis) she cut the thread.

Hades- the god of the Underworld. After the war between the Olympians and Titans, he was chosen to oversee the realm of the dead. In mythology, he stole Persephone from a flower field and she is forced to spend half the year with him.

Hector- a Trojan prince, son of Priam and Hecuba, and notably the greatest fighter for Troy. He was killed in a duel with Achilles and subsequently, dragged behind his chariot back to the Grecian camps.

Hecuba- queen of Troy and wife of Priam. When the Greeks eventually destroyed her city, she was forced to look upon her dead children and grandchildren before being enslaved as a spoil of war. Her most notable children include Hector, Paris and Cassandra.

Helen- a demigoddess identified by Aphrodite to be the most beautiful woman in the world. In myth, she stole away with Paris back to Troy for unclear reasons. Some accounts say she was kidnapped, while others say she chose to leave her husband, Menelaus. Her departure from Sparta ignited the Trojan War, most notably depicted in Homer's Iliad.

Heracles- the son of Zeus who was renowned for his super human strength. At birth, Hera tried to kill him by sending snakes after him, but he strangled them. Later in life, Hera sent him into a blind rage, where he murders his wife and children. From this we have the labors of Heracles, a series of impossible tasks his king half-brother sends him on. These trials include slaying the Nemean Lion, slaying the Hydra, stealing the apples of Hesperides, and capturing Cerberus and delivering him from the underworld to his half-brother.

Hubris- in Greek mythology it referred to a hero's greatest flaw, which offended the gods and would ultimately lead to the hero's demise.

Medusa- a former priestess of Athena. She was brutally raped by Poseidon in Athena's temple. For the disgrace, Athena transformed her into a Gorgon. If anyone laid eyes on her, they were turned into stone.

She was eventually killed by Perseus, as he was tasked to retrieve her head in exchange for his mother's return.

Menelaus- king of Sparta and former husband to Helen. His brother, Agamemnon led the Trojan War to restore his honor. His story is told in Homer's Iliad and Odyssey.

The Minotaur- the half-man half-bull, flesh eating beast that was slain by Theseus, with aid by Ariadne, in the myth of the labyrinth.

Mnemosyne- the goddess of memory and mother of the nine Muses.

The Muses- the nine daughters of Zeus and Mnemosyne which personified arts and culture. Calliope was the muse of epic poetry. Clio, muse of history. Euterpe, muse of lyric poetry. Thalia, muse of comedy. Melpomene, muse of tragedy. Terpsichore, muse of dance. Erato, muse of love poems. Polyhymnia, muse of sacred poetry. Urania, muse of astronomy.

The Myrmidons- the army led by Achilles. In some accounts they were a super army created by Zeus out of ants and others account them as being a special army trained personally by Achilles, either way their name comes from the Greek word meaning ant.

Nymphs- a term for a lesser goddess.

Odysseus/ Ulysses- one of the many Greek heroes to fight for Menelaus in the Trojan War. He was notable for his plan and execution of the Trojan Horse. Homer's Odyssey follows his perilous journey back home to his kingdom of Ithaca, after the war.

Olympus- the mountain palace of the gods, specifically the Olympians.

Orion- a great hunter who was slain by a scorpion sent by Gaia, since she felt he would go on to kill every beast on the planet if no one stopped him. His body was placed among the stars by Zeus on request of his friend, Artemis.

Pan- god of the wild, nature (specifically mountains,) shepherds. He is typically depicted as a Satyr (a half-man half-goat being) and was often considered a companion to nymphs in Greek mythology.

Paris- a prince of Troy most notable in mythology for stealing away Helen from Sparta and igniting the war between the kingdoms of Greece and the city of Troy.

Pasiphae- daughter of the sun god, Helios, who engaged in sex with the sacred sun bull and subsequently birthed the half-man half-bull, flesh eating monster known as the Minotaur.

Patroclus- lover of Achilles who died a tragic death sparking his revengeful return to battle to defeat Hector in hand to hand combat and enact the prophecy of Achilles' downfall.

Priam- king of Troy. His most notable children were Hector, Paris and Cassandra.

Psyche- a mortal princess turned goddess of the soul. In mythology, she was sacrificed to marry a mysterious monster who came to her each night under the cover of darkness. Out of curiosity, one night she lit a candle, only to find it was the god Cupid sleeping beside her. She was then cursed to walk the world until her death, where Cupid came to her again and for her devotion to him, made her a goddess. She is personified by the butterfly.

Selene- goddess of the moon.

Zeus/Jove- the god of the sky and thunder. He led the revolution to free his siblings from the belly of his father, Cronus. With aid from some Titans, the Olympians won the war. This solidified Zeus as king of all gods. In mythology, Zeus is often seen as unfaithful to his wife (and sister) Hera. Many of the gods and heroes in Grecian myth are his children by another woman, much to Hera's displeasure. This is the crux of many conflicts in Grecian mythology.

Judeo Christian

Adam- in the Judeo-Christian world origin story, he was the first human created by Yahweh (otherwise known as God.) Accounts say that he was molded out of clay in God's image. In early Judaism, Adam had a first wife, Lilith, who was also molded out of clay. His second wife, Eve, however was constructed from one of Adam's rib.

Delilah- in the biblical story of Samson, she betrays his love by having a servant cut his hair, which held the power of his strength. After being stripped his power, she gave him over to his enemies (the Philistines) who then mutilated him, only to then force him to work in a grain mill. The story between her and Samson can be found in the Book of Judges.

Judas Iscariot- One of the original disciples of Jesus. In the bible, Judas betrayed Jesus by identifying him with a kiss, thus giving him away to the Romans who would later crucify him. The reasons for his betrayal have been debated, but in the Gospel of Matthew, it is indicated that he was financially compensated for the betrayal.

Israel- the name God gave Jacob after having received a blessing from the angel he tackled in the Jacob's Ladder story, which can be found in the Book of Genesis. He was the son of Isaac and brother to Esau. He had twelve sons (Reuben, Simeon, Levi, Judah, Dan, Naphtali, Gad, Asher, Issachar, Zebulun, Joseph, Benjamin) and one (recorded, there were probably more) daughter, Dinah, by his two wives, Leah and

Rachel and their handmaids. He is attributed to be the patriarch of the Tribes of Israel.

Mary- in Catholic mythology, she was the virgin mother of Christ the savior.

Moses- in an act of divine intervention, he was saved as an infant and safely carried down the Nile River to the home of the Pharaohs, after his mother prayed to god for his safe deliverance and escape from the Jewish persecution in Egypt. His basket was found by Pharaoh Rameses I's wife and he was taken in as an adoptive child. As an adult, he learned of his Jewish heritage (after having met his biological siblings, Miriam and Aaron,) which led him to embark on a spiritual journey which brought him closer to god. God, in the form of a burning bush, eventually speaks to Moses and instructs him to liberate his people enslaved in Egypt. His confrontation with Pharaoh Rameses II ultimately leads to the ten plagues of Egypt, ending in Moses parting the Red Sea to continue the journey of delivering his people to the promise land. His story can be found in the book of Exodus.

Samson- a heroic figure which divine-like strength granted to him through his uncut hair. He was ultimately betrayed by his lover, Delilah, who cut his hair, stripping him of his super human strength and turned him over to his enemies. His eyes were gouged out and he was forced to work a grain mill. After much prayer, he was granted his strength back and tore down the columns of the Temple of Dagon, killing himself and his captors.

Acknowledgements

I would like to thank the following for their continued support. In one way or another, you helped propel this book into existence, so thank you.

Jac Shacter, the greatest love I know (besides the girls, obviously.) Thank you for your continued enthusiasm and willingness to read my poetry, even when you don't understand half the mythological references, even when it's 2am and you have work in the morning, even when you've heard the same poem more than once. Thank you for supporting me at open mic events. Thank you for helping and supporting me in my nonprofit work. Thank you for being open to new experiences even when you could probably care less about poetry. I really don't know anyone else who would willingly read through my glossary for missing info other than you. I guess, that just shows how much you love me.

Yolanda Bradley, thank you for continuing to support my books. I don't know anyone more insistent that I sign their copy of my book than you. You're the best.

Mom & Dad, thank you for everything you have done, and continue to do, for me and the girls. I hope you know, your love has not gone unnoticed.

To the rest of my family, thank you for your continuous support. It means so much to hear you all cheer me on across the country. From Homer, Alaska to Brooklyn, NYC, thank you for celebrating this with me.

Madeline Windsor & Stephen Stokes, thank you both for offering your time to read my work. Your critiques stick with me and I keep them in consideration whenever I'm writing.

and finally,
        J.F.R.
Thank you for showing me what a person should not be. Your lack of integrity has sent me on a journey of personal growth. I would say, without you these books wouldn't exist, but I firmly believe if I had never met you, I would have published a lot sooner. I remember you so clearly discouraging me from writing. How you would say I could never write a book. How you even said my writing sucked. Makes me wonder if you were afraid of what I would write- how I would write you.
        So thanks, asshole.
        Thanks for being you.

About the Author

Dakota Boyer is a poet residing in Northern Florida or, as some people in her area would refer to it, South Georgia. When she's not writing, Dakota is eager to slip fun facts into every day conversation, read the next book on her ever growing to be read list, create blackout poetry, engage in the local art scene and play make believe with her toddlers.

From a Vein of Lapis Lazuli is her third collection, following Of Violent Delights and Edge of Stardust, but this is her first collection featuring prose and short fiction alongside poetry.

You can find her on Instagram @thunderousdandelion.

Made in the USA
Columbia, SC
11 January 2025

50553324R00071